MOTHERHOOD OUT LOUD

WRITTEN BY
LESLIE AYVAZIAN, BROOKE BERMAN,
DAVID CALE, JESSICA GOLDBERG,
BETH HENLEY, LAMEECE ISSAQ,
CLAIRE LaZEBNIK, LISA LOOMER,
MICHELE LOWE, MARCO PENNETTE,
THERESA REBECK, LUANNE RICE,
ANNIE WEISMAN AND CHERYL L. WEST

CONCEIVED BY
SUSAN R. ROSE AND JOAN STEIN

★

DRAMATISTS
PLAY SERVICE
INC.

MOTHERHOOD OUT LOUD
Copyright © 2012, Susan R. Rose and Ted Weiant

All Rights Reserved

SPECIAL NOTE

MOTHERHOOD OUT LOUD
written by Leslie Ayvazian, Brooke Berman, David Cale, Jessica Goldberg,
Beth Henley, Lameece Issaq, Claire LaZebnik, Lisa Loomer, Michele Lowe,
Marco Pennette, Theresa Rebeck, Luanne Rice, Anne Weisman and Cheryl L. West

Conceived by Susan R. Rose and Joan Stein

MOTHERHOOD OUT LOUD was developed by Susan R. Rose and Joan Stein
with the support of Renee Landegger, Judith Resnick, Jonathan Murray,
Rodger Hess, and Robin Gorman Newman.

World Premiere presented by Hartford Stage, Hartford, Connecticut.

New York Premiere presented by Primary Stages, New York City.

Dedicated to my friend and co-creator Joan Stein

PRODUCTION NOTE

MOTHERHOOD OUT LOUD can be presented as a reading, with scripts on music stands, or it can be fully staged. The play can involve as many actors as you choose, and as few as four — three women and one man. If the production is presented with four actors, these are the role assignments for each:

ACTOR A: New in the Motherhood; Baby Bird (Woman); Michael's Date; Bridal Shop; My Baby

ACTOR B: Squeeze, Hold, Release; Baby Bird (Stranger/Strange Kid); Nooha's List; Bridal Shop; Stars and Stripes; Report on Motherhood (Great-Granddaughter)

ACTOR C: Next to the Crib; Queen Esther; My Almost Family; Threesome; Report on Motherhood (Great-Grandmother)

ACTOR D: If We're Using a Surrogate …; Threesome; Elizabeth

MOTHERHOOD OUT LOUD received its Off-Broadway premiere at Primary Stages on October 4, 2011. It was directed by Lisa Peterson; the set design was by Rachel Hauck; the sound design was by Jill BC Duboff; the costume design was by David C. Woolard; the projection design was by Jan Hartley; the animation design was by Emily Hubley; and the production stage manager was Donald Fried. The cast featured Mary Bacon, Saidah Arrika Ekulona, Randy Graff and James Lecesne.

SCENES

CHAPTER ONE: FAST BIRTHS

FAST BIRTHS FUGUE — Michele Lowe

SQUEEZE, HOLD, RELEASE — Cheryl L. West

NEXT TO THE CRIB — Brooke Berman

NEW IN THE MOTHERHOOD — Lisa Loomer

CHAPTER TWO: FIRST DAY

FIRST DAY FUGUE — Michele Lowe

QUEEN ESTHER — Michele Lowe

BABY BIRD — Theresa Rebeck

IF WE'RE USING A SURROGATE , HOW COME I'M
THE ONE WITH MORNING SICKNESS — Marco Pennette

CHAPTER THREE: SEX TALK

SEX TALK FUGUE — Michele Lowe

NOOHA'S LIST — Lameece Issaq

MY ALMOST FAMILY — Luanne Rice

MICHAEL'S DATE — Claire LaZebnik

CHAPTER FOUR: STEPPING OUT

GRADUATION DAY FUGUE — Michele Lowe

THREESOME — Leslie Ayvazian

BRIDAL SHOP — Michele Lowe

STARS AND STRIPES — Jessica Goldberg

CHAPTER FIVE: COMING HOME

THANKSGIVING FUGUE — Michele Lowe

ELIZABETH — David Cale

REPORT ON MOTHERHOOD — Beth Henley

MY BABY — Annie Weisman

MOTHERHOOD OUT LOUD

CHAPTER ONE: FAST BIRTHS

FAST BIRTHS FUGUE
by Michele Lowe

Three actresses, A, B, C.

A. I go into premature labor and my doctor puts me on an IV that makes me feel like I've just had fifty-six espressos …

B. I'm in the back seat of the station wagon on all fours panting like a dog …

A. After two weeks the doctor says, "I can take you off the drugs tomorrow but if you go into labor I'm going to be way out on Exit 51 on the L.I.E. for Thanksgiving, so if you wouldn't mind can we wait a day?"

C. This Japanese doctor has Ben's head by the forceps and he jumps on my belly to get a better grip …

B. They finally give me my epidural and a lollipop and I'm thinking, "Where the fuck is the Jack Daniels?"

A. The nurse comes in and I say, "I feel something happening." She looks at the monitor on my belly and says, "Nope. Not yet."

C. I'm pushing like crazy but every time I stop the baby gets sucked back inside because the umbilical cord is wrapped around his neck …

A. The nurse comes in again and I say, "Look, I think I'm having contractions." She checks the monitor and says, "Nope. Not yet."

B. I don't know what's fucking happening to me, I didn't take any muthafucking baby class, I think my body's gonna split in two and I start screaming …
C. This woman is screaming in the hall …
A. The nurse comes in again and I'm in agony and I say, "Look lady, I'm having contractions." Another nurse comes in behind her. Looks at my belly and says to her, "You've got the monitor upside down."
B. Billions of women have done this, right?
A. I'm praying.
B. I'm panting.
C. I'm pushing.
A. He's my fifth.
B. My first.
C. My third.
A. Oh my God.
C. I think my third.
B. One more push —
C. One more —
A. Whatever you do, don't stop —
C. Here he comes!
ALL. Holy shiiit! *(Lights shift.)*

SQUEEZE, HOLD, RELEASE
by Cheryl L. West

Oh, good Lord! Now what? Why won't she just get in the damn car and just go? You age ten years on one of my mother's goodbyes and she's in rare form today. After all, she's saying her first goodbye to her first grandchild, my five-day-old little precious. "You're a mother now," my mother sings, punching my dad in the arm so he'll come in on the chorus, *(Singing.)* "You're in the motherhood club now — your life will never be the same." *(Daughter waves.)* "Bye-bye, Mom. Dad. Yes, it's been great. Couldn't have done it without you. Yes, I'll miss you, too! No, miss you more." My husband cranks the engine, and just as I think I'm finally free, she jumps out the car waving a bunch of photos. Dammit, now what? "Look at this picture! How many kids do you see there? Four. Four children! That's right. Popped out all four of you. No drugs, no science fiction shots to my back ... barely an ouch uttered from my throat. The nurses all wanted to give me an award for being the most silent mother to be." "And you've been making up for lost time ever since." "But my point is, honey, motherhood is suffering, most times in silence, and you just can't operate the same ass backwards way anymore." "Remember, Mom, I'm the one who planned for motherhood!" "Planning is for shit, Smartie Pants. God favors your child over you now. So plan on that! Your heart's about to get broken every which way but loose." Watching her eyes brim with tears, I'm starting to feel maybe her staying another day wouldn't be so bad ... "Mom, is there anything that I should know, that maybe I haven't thought about?" Wrong move. "Gentlemen, close your ears. CLOSE 'EM! Okay, honey, here goes: Men like to pause at the doorway; not fall through it! So, whatever you do, get that little doorway tight again. Swaddle the little precious, but there's a bigger precious that needs swaddling, too. Tight, if you know what I mean." It's simple, dear: Squeeze, hold, release! That's what mothers do, all day long, everyday: Squeeze, hold, release!" "Four kids and forty-five years later, I can still cradle a dumbbell up there for an hour if I had to ... Got a bladder like a steel drum. Now that's what you call a mother that's still a woman!" That's it! My husband decides my sanity has been held hostage long enough. He finally gets Mom to put two feet in his car and whisks her and Dad off to the airport, leaving me standing there waving *(Waves.)* ... feeling lonelier than I ever have in my life. "Bye-bye Mom. Bye-bye." Wishing ... yes, wishing I could call her back ... But I can't, so guess what I find myself doing? Squeeze, hold, release. *(The baby gurgles.)* Maybe your grandmother was right! *(She gives the baby a big kiss.)* Maybe that's the definition of motherhood. You do squeeze your child, and you hold on to them tight, and yes, eventually one day you release them out into the world ... But not, not today ... not today. *(She grins, excited as the newly anointed usually are.)* Yes, SQUEEZE, HOLD, RELEASE! *(The baby starts to cry. She panics.)* Oh-oh! Now what, mother?

NEXT TO THE CRIB
by Brooke Berman

A woman spreads a sheet on the floor, lies down on it and attempts to get comfortable. It's hard. The floor is not comfortable. She tries again. She sits up.

WOMAN. This is me. On the floor. Next to my baby's crib. My baby is a sleep terrorist, waking every two hours to feed. All day — and all night long. Tonight, I'm horizontal on shitty carpeting, nestled between the crib and changing table, because my husband has a cold. A cold! "Don't do any night-feedings." I said. "Rest." This made me look like a very loving wife. But I am saving my own neck. I am not getting sick. My baby is not getting sick. And I am not getting sick. Stay the fuck away from us. *(She spreads her blankets out on the floor, creating a nest. She tries to lie down and sleep. She cannot. She gets back up and talks to us again.)* I used to be an insomniac. I spent a great portion of the last decade not sleeping. So I thought the "sleep deprivation" part of motherhood would be easy. I love 2 A.M.! I'd stumble into some all night diner from some dance club and eat French fries. Or sit awake at home enjoying the quiet. "I am a 2 A.M. kind of girl! I won't mind four-hour nights! I can totally function on four hours of sleep!" Fuck that. Sleep deprivation is killing me. Sometimes, when I'm leaving the house, I turn to my husband and ask, "Do I look okay? Or like a crazy person?" And sometimes he doesn't answer. In "Mommy and Me" class, I learned about something called "The Four Month Sleep Regression." (Technically, they'd have to be "sleeping" in order to "regress" – but … whatever.) Apparently, at four months, any progress you've made teaching them to sleep goes out the window. And then TEETHING! Followed by crawling and then separation anxiety. All of which keep them awake. When do they sleep!? When do I?!? *(She tries to lie down and sleep. It doesn't work. And she's up, addressing the audience again.)* I saw this play about Romania just before the revolution. I bet those characters could sleep on the floor. Those characters, hungry and clad in gray, would know how to fall asleep on this carpeting without creature comforts. Creature comforts do not exist when you're overthrowing a Communist regime! Or, maybe we're escaping Nazi Germany, hiding on all sorts of floors as we make our way to the border, like the pianist in *The Pianist*. Or, camping! I've gone camping. In a dense forest. And the tents are inadequate and the ground is cold, and there is nothing resembling a coffee shop anywhere. … Oh my God, what if we get eaten by bears!? *(Giving up as the fantasy collapses. From the other room, we hear her husband's very loud sneeze or nose-blowing, sounds of a bad cold.)*

If I get sick I will kill him with these very hands. And if my baby gets sick, I will kill him and then myself.

Maybe I'm not cut out for this. I have spent the last 20 years as an adult doing whatever I wanted to do whenever I wanted to do it — and that's over. FOREVER. Never again will I move through the world without care. FOREVER, and I mean forever, there will be this tie, the thought, "Where's my kid? Is my kid okay?"

I belong to him now. With my husband I can at least pretend some kind of emotional autonomy, like that Rilkean sort of "two solitudes that border each other" bullshit. But with my baby? Uh-uh, no way, it's full-on. He depends on me. And I better be up to the task … Or else. *(Lights out.)*

NEW IN THE MOTHERHOOD
by Lisa Loomer

A woman walks on with a happy looking diaper bag. She's kind of an odd mom out. Not sarcastic ... a bit bewildered and wry. She's fine with the kid, easy ... The rest of her new life she's still trying to figure out.

ODD MOM. *(To audience.)* Oh, hi. This bench taken? *(Sits.)* Cool. *(Sees son, calls out; lightly.)* Put it down, Harry. Down, babe. The tricycle is a means of transportation. *(Laughs.)* He's three. Everything's a penis. *(She takes out a cigarette.)* God, I hate the park. If anyone had told me I'd be sentenced to five to ten years in the park ... I'd have stuck with a cat. *(Re: cigarette.)* Oh, this is clove by the way. *(Takes a drag.)* All right, it's not clove, but it's the park. See, the park for me is like ... Dante's Purgatory. Not Dante's Inferno — that'd be exciting, you'd meet interesting people ... But, I mean, day after day of whose turn is it on the swing? Couldn't we just let 'em duke it out? I mean, I used to go to an office ... Like — in a building? I was a type A personality! Okay, B minus, but still ... *(Takes a drag; smiles.)* Look, I know he's a boy, you gotta take 'em outside. They will not play Scrabble. They'll throw the pieces at the cat. And they won't miss, 'cause they're boys. *(Lightly.)* And you can't just let his dad take him to the park, 'cause, hey — "Where was Mom? Working?" He'll be in therapy the rest of his life — *(Notices; matter of fact.)* Harry? No, honey — put the little girl down. Put her down, babe. *(Waits; easy.)* Put her down and use your words, Harry. *(Beat.)* Not those words — *(Laughs.)* Hey, remind me to cancel Showtime — ! *(Mom 1 enters, startling her. She's perfect. And eight months pregnant.)*
MOM 1. *(Perky.)* Excuse me, is anybody sitting there?
ODD MOM. *(Trying for cheery.)* Oh no! *(Odd Mom moves over.)*
MOM 1. I love your diaper bag!
ODD MOM. Yours, too! *(Mom 1 looks at the cigarette and coughs meaningfully.)* Oh, don't worry about this, it's clove. *(Mom 1 calls to her child on the swings — near Harry.)*

MOM 1. Dakota! Just tell the little boy, "Go away." Do not let him do that with your Barbie! *(To Odd Mom.)* Must be one of the nannies' kids. But I think it's good ours get to negotiate with all kinds, don't you?

ODD MOM. *(To audience.)* And because hell's not an issue for me, I say — *(To Mom 1.)* Sure! *(Mom 2 enters. Perky. She spots Mom 1.)*

MOM 2. *(High-pitched.)* Hi!

MOM 1. *(High-pitched.)* Hi!

ODD MOM. *(To audience.)* Lower register's completely shot. Minute the baby drops —

MOM 2. *(To Odd Mom.)* I love your diaper bag!

ODD MOM. *(Trying for high-pitched.)* Yours, too!

MOM 2. *(Sits; to Mom 1.)* Say, can Dakota have a playdate with Orleans today?

ODD MOM. *(To audience; just doesn't get it.)* The playdate. Don't they have enough fun in the park? The playdate is like the park — only in your house. The playdate, for a boy, is like, "I've already broken all my stuff, now I get to break yours!" Still, I kinda hope they invite us ...

MOM 1. *(To Mom 2.)* How's twelve?

MOM 2. Great! I can make gyrotonics!

ODD MOM. *(Trying to join in.)* I can make gin and tonics — *(The Moms smile or ignore her and continue to each other ...)*

MOM 1. *(Pats her tummy.)* I just pray these two sleep through the night so I have the energy for class.

MOM 2. Well, I hope you're going to Ferberize them!

ODD MOM. *(Trying to follow.)* Ferberize ... Now is that the sleep book that says if she cries don't pick her up? Ever? Like — just let her scream while you watch *The Colbert Report*?

MOM 2. It's about letting them self-soothe.

MOM 1. I wish we'd Ferberized Dakota, I can't even get her off the pacifier!

ODD MOM. Have you tried sugar on your finger? *(The other mothers gasp audibly.)*

MOM 2. *(To Mom 1.)* Let's do the playdate at our house; they can do an art project with the nanny.

MOM 1. Great. Ours is hopeless at art —

ODD MOM. Oh God, me too. I suck at art. Costumes ... masks ... to me, papier-mâché is like ... vomit. *(That's it. The Moms look at their watches and rise.)*

MOM 1. Well, will you look at the time?! *(Calls out.)* Dakota! Take back your doll and tell the little boy good-bye. *(Panicking.)* Dakota — NO! DON'T USE HIS SIPPY CUP! DO NOT USE HIS SIPPY CUP!

MOM 2. DON'T TOUCH THAT SIPPY CUP!

MOM 1. Dakota — !

MOM 2. *(Low voice; "drop that gun.")* Orleans, drop the sippy cup. Now. *(Screams.)* DROP THAT SIPPY CUP!

MOM 1. *(To Mom 2.)* HE'S PROBABLY NOT EVEN VACCINATED!

ODD MOM. *(Simply.)* Dammit, Harry, just take your sippy cup and give back the Michelle Obama Barbie. *(The Moms look at her. She looks at them. Unrepentant.)*

MOM 2. *(Smiles.)* Well.

MOM 1. *(What can she say?)* Great diaper bag! *(They hurry off.)*

ODD MOM. *(Looks after them.)* Bite me. *(To audience.)* Man, I love my kid … But sometimes I wish we'd met under different circumstances. Really, the only upside to all this is … *(Sees Harry; smiles.)* Him. So here's what they don't tell you in *What To Expect When You're Expecting* … *(Looks after Moms.)* Expect to hope that people you don't like will invite you to reptile birthday parties. *(Puts out cigarette.)* Expect to give up smoking — eventually — because you can't bear to breathe secondary smoke on him. Expect to be unable to not open letters from UNICEF, and Greenpeace, and even Smile Train — because it's his world now. Expect to cry in the aisles of Rite Aid when he's sick and pray to a God you don't believe in to make him well. Just make him a happy, healthy kid! *(Can't resist.)* And a Democrat. A real one. Hey, Harry? Let's go get a doughnut, babe. Above all, expect to come back to the park tomorrow with juice boxes and cookies, and fucking bake 'em if you have to — *(To audience.)* See you tomorrow! *(Lights shift.)*

CHAPTER TWO: FIRST DAY

FIRST DAY FUGUE
by Michele Lowe

B. First day of school.

A. Six hours to myself for the first time in a decade. Somebody pinch me.

C. I'm supposed to drop off my daughter in front of school and not go inside. They tell me this in a letter.

B. I tell Katie, "When you get to the front door, baby, you wave and I'll wave and I'll catch your wave and you catch my wave."

C. What do you mean I can't go into my kid's school? Jessica's four years old. If I want to walk her in, that's my prerogative. I'm her mother.

B. And she says "Momma, don't forget to catch my wave. I'm gonna wave real big to you."

A. My son Peter sneezes. I wonder if he's catching a cold. I make him get on the bus anyway.

B. Katie gets to the door, and all these kids are surging into the school, and she disappears. She's gone. No wave. Nothing.

A. Then I go running up to my bedroom and I take off all my clothes. I text my husband. "Darling, there's a naked woman in our bed. What're you gonna do about it?"

C. I march into school past this mother who's waving like crazy, like she's landing an airplane, and the principal says to Jessica, "Hello, my dear. Why don't you come with me?" My dear my ass. She's not going with him. But Jessica lets go of me and takes his hand.

A. My father-in-law texts me back: "Sounds good to me."

B. Five minutes later, I'm still standing there outside the school. The kids have all gone in but I'm still waving, waving at the door, I swear I am, 'til a woman comes over to me and says, "You get over it." She's really young, and I know she means well, but I still tell her, "Lady, that's my fifth child who just walked in there, and I will never get over it." *(Lights shift.)*

QUEEN ESTHER
by Michele Lowe

I pick up Sammy at Lois Baum's house — he plays with her daughter Amy on Thursdays when I work late — and as he's putting on his boots, Lois pulls me aside and says, "You know, Purim's in a few weeks, and the kids want to get dressed up in costumes for the Megillah reading at temple." And I say, "Oh great, we'll have to get something," and she says, "Listen I don't know how to tell you this but your son already has something in mind. He wants to go as Queen Esther. He told me he wants to wear a wedding dress. Look," she says, "we don't know each other that well, but I love my pediatrician and he might be very good for you right now. He's very empathic." She hands me a piece of paper with the doctor's telephone number on it and Sammy and I leave. When Sammy was three, he wanted a Cinderella dress from the Disney Store. It was two shades of blue with a little cap sleeve. We told the salesclerk it was a birthday gift for a little girl in his class, but when we got home, he put it on. He wore it every night for three weeks and then I shredded it in the washing machine. He never mentioned the dress again and neither did I. When he was five my mother bought him a Buzz Lightyear costume for Halloween. He begged me to take it back and buy him a Sleeping Beauty dress. I couldn't. All this time Sammy's father is trying to find Sammy a sport. Every other weekend he's all over Sammy, "This is how you throw a football, this is how you hit a forehand, this is how you dribble a basketball." Sammy's coming home with a broken finger, a twisted ankle, a bloody nose, but he never complains. I call Sammy's father and ask if he could tone down the ESPN lessons but he laughs at me. "He likes it," he says. "He's gonna be the next Derek Jeter." And I think, sure — if Derek Jeter likes to wear a little black dress and pearls. So after my conversation with Lois I decide to skip Purim this year. I tell Sammy, "We'll bake hammantaschen and go visit Gramma." Sammy loves to bake and he says, "Fine." So the costume thing goes away. A few days later, Sammy comes home with a huge black and

16

blue mark on his arm. He tells me he walked into the art cabinet. I get a phone call from his teacher — Sammy isn't participating in class anymore. Sammy's getting into fights. Sammy's sitting by himself at recess. Then I get a call from Sammy's father. Sammy won't eat. Sammy looks miserable. Sammy's not happy. Then the son of a bitch says maybe we should revisit our custody agreement because it's obvious something's not right and I hang up on him which is a bad move because he can use that in court against me. That night as Sammy's getting into bed I say, "Hey buddy, I got a call from Mrs. McCarthy. She says you're not really being yourself." And he asks, "What's being myself?" And I say, "Being the way you are deep down — a good kid, a confident kid, a happy kid." And he says, "Mommy, I just don't feel like myself right now." And I say, "You don't feel like yourself?" He says, "No, I don't feel like me." Now, the kid is seven years old and I'm listening to what I think is psychobabble he's heard on the radio but he continues — "You know what would help?" "What, Sam?" "A barrette in my hair." "A barrette?" "Yes. That and a pair of high heels. I want to dress up as Queen Esther for Purim." "Why Esther? Why do you want to go as Esther?" "Because the King was going to kill all the Jews and Esther told him if he did that he'd have to kill her too. And the King loved Esther more than anybody." "Can't you go as Mordecai, Esther's cousin? He was there." "But she was the one willing to sacrifice everything to change the King's mind. Mama she did the right thing." I don't sleep all night. My kid really wants this and if I pass judgment on him, what's everybody else going to do? So I go to the Disney Store and I buy him the Sleeping Beauty dress — pink sparkle fake organza — and I have it waiting for him when he gets home from school. He runs upstairs and puts it on and calls me to come look at him and — and — he looks great. It looks like him. The way he was supposed to be — like a girl. That night we walk into temple and there are three, maybe four hundred people looking for seats. All the girls are dressed like Sammy and all the boys are dressed as Mordecai with ninja swords and headbands. Right away, anyone who recognizes Sammy stares. I look straight ahead. I don't make eye contact with any of them. Meanwhile Sammy's having the time of his life; he's spinning in his dress, he's comparing heel heights with a little girl. There are no seats left so we have to sit in the front pew. I start praying: *Dear God, give me a sign. Tell me I haven't totally screwed him up by letting him come here like this.* I hear people behind us whispering and I think maybe Sammy can take it, but I can't. We have to get out of here. But the service starts and we're trapped. The woman next to me gets a good look at Sammy and I hear her whisper to her husband, "Look at that little boy: he's wearing a dress. A dress!" I look over at Sammy and the barrette has slipped and fallen in his lap. He's pulling the elastic on the sleeves because it's too tight on his arms. "Do I look all right, Mama?" He asks. "Tell me the truth." I can feel him shaking. He heard what that woman next to us said. He hears them whispering behind us. I pick up his barrette and clip it back into his hair and then I put my arm around him and I feel him relax into me. He fits right inside my waist near my hip. We are one again, him and me. We are Esther and the King and we are invincible. *(Lights shift.)*

BABY BIRD
by Theresa Rebeck

A woman.

WOMAN. Sometimes when they meet my daughter people say —
STRANGER. Why hello! What's your name?
WOMAN. And my daughter tells her name, Cleo, that's her name, Cleo. Then sometimes these people say to me —
STRANGER. She's so beautiful
WOMAN. And I say, thank you.
STRANGER. Where is she from?
WOMAN. China, I say.
STRANGER. Are you teaching her Chinese?
WOMAN. Somehow this is a big concern to everyone, that I teach my daughter Chinese. No, I say.
STRANGER. Oh.
WOMAN. Not yet!

STRANGER. *(Feeling a little better.)* Oh.

WOMAN. Sometimes, if this person has adopted a daughter from China herself, she says —

STRANGER. *(Judgmental.)* Do you teach her anything about China?

WOMAN. And I say, yes, of course! We have thousands of books about China and Chinese art on the walls and we watch *Mulan* like all the time. Alllll the time. And then because I still feel bad, what kind of a bad mother would adopt a kid from China and then not teach her Chinese, Mandarin is actually the appropriate response, MANDARIN, I sometimes say, "My son is, I have a son, Cooper, who is twelve, and he's biological, and you know, if we taught my daughter Chinese but didn't have Cooper learn Chinese as well, it would be like, he's our biological kid, and she's our Chinese kid, and we don't want to do that." *(Pause.)* This answer invariably gives people allllll sorts of permission.

STRANGER. Your son is biological?

WOMAN. Yes.

STRANGER. If you have a biological child, why did you adopt?

WOMAN. Okay I hate this question, and by this point I hate this person, but, oh well, what can you do. Everyone is always so polite. *(To Stranger.)* It was just something we wanted to do.

STRANGER. Do they get along?

WOMAN. What?

STRANGER. Your son and your daughter, do they get along?

WOMAN. Okay. "Do your son and daughter get along?" Would you say this to anyone with a normal family? Wait a minute. My family is a normal family. *(Then.)* Yes, they get along! Most of the time.

STRANGER. *(A little too patronizing.)* Isn't that great. Did you go to China to get her?

WOMAN. Where else would we get her? She's Chinese. *(Then.)* Yes, we did!

STRANGER. Did your son go with you?

WOMAN. Yes, he did.

STRANGER. That must have been a wonderful experience for him!

WOMAN. Actually, he got kind of sick of it. There was one point when Cooper actually refused to get off the bus. We went to a famous Chinese museum where they had cool dioramas of Lord Bao, who was a famous court advisor to some emperor, and Cooper was so sick of being dragged all over China in a bus with twenty stressed-out parents and ten freaked-out Chinese babies that he actually just said, "No, I REFUSE to get off the bus." Those were his words, "I REFUSE." I had to get back on the bus and tell him if he didn't get off the damn bus I would not buy him Yu-gi-oh cards when we got to Guangjho, a city where, we had been told, the streets are PAVED with Yu-gi-oh cards. This threat actually got my sweet son to get off the stupid bus. *(To Stranger.)* Yes, he loved it!

STRANGER. Well, isn't that interesting. A biological child AND an adopted Chinese daughter. Good for you. Good for you!

WOMAN. Thank you? *(Then.)* This is what kids say:

STRANGE KID. He can't be her brother.

WOMAN. Of course he's her brother.

STRANGE KID. They don't look alike. How can he be her brother?

WOMAN. *(Pissed.)* She's adopted.

STRANGE KID. Adopted? What does that mean?

WOMAN. Okay, who are the parents out there who have not explained ADOPTION to their kids at this point? Could I have a word with you? Could you please explain to them that families come together in different ways, and not all babies come out of the tummies of the mommies who are their real mommies? Could I not be expected to explain this to strange children on the playground, in front of my own child, who gets a little confused and freaked out when kids say this in front of her? *(To strange kid.)* You know what? Maybe you could go ask your mommy about adoption.

STRANGE KID. I know what adoption is. It means you're not her real mom.

WOMAN. Go away. Go away! *(Strange kid goes away.)*

STRANGER. Your daughter is from China but your son is biological? So it's not that you're infertile.

WOMAN. I don't want to talk about my fertility with NEAR STRANGERS.

STRANGER. Your daughter is Chinese but your son is biological? How is that working out for you?

WOMAN. We're the same as every other family.

STRANGER. Well, you know, actually — no. You're not. *(Beat.)*

WOMAN. You know I was, actually, there was one day when Cleo told me she was worried about all the other babies in China. She was four at the time, and she was worried that their parents would not find them, the way we had found her. So I told her that the Chinese government was very good, very efficient, and that they knew how to get the right babies to the right parents. Which made her feel better, but I did realize that she thought that that was where all babies came from — orphanages in China. I worried about this for weeks. My husband finally said, "What are you so worried about?" And I said, "I am going to have to tell her that some babies come out of their mother's stomachs. And that, in fact, her brother came out of my stomach, and she did not, she came out of another woman's stomach, in China. Don't you think that will upset her?" And my husband said, "Well, no babies come out of my stomach, so I never actually thought about it." *(Then.)* I did tell her. That sometimes babies came out of their mommy's stomachs. She thought this was hilarious; she laughed and laughed. So I said, "Yes that is funny, but you know, your brother came out of my stomach." Which gave her pause. And then she said, "I wish I came out of your stomach." So we talked about it for a little, and she went off to play. Then that night, when I was putting her to bed, she said to me, "You know what I wish? I wish Cooper came from China." And I said, "Yes, that would be the other way to level the playing field. But whether or not you came out of my stomach, you are my baby bird, and I am your mother." *(Then.)* Which somehow seems to work for her, and me, and her brother, and her father. It really does. *(Lights shift.)*

IF WE'RE USING A SURROGATE, HOW COME I'M THE ONE WITH MORNING SICKNESS?
by Marco Pennette

Holiday Muzak plays in the darkness. A department store. Lights up on a Man holding shopping bags filled with presents. Santa Claus is in the distance. He suddenly turns to us, frustrated.

MAN.   Un-fucking-believable. First words out of his mouth — "Have you been a good girl for mommy?" *(Shakes his head.)* Why am I surprised? They all say it — waitresses, salespeople. "Where's your mommy?" "Is Daddy giving Mommy a break?" Why should Santa be any different? But instead of pretending I didn't hear it, I turn to him and yell, "Hey, fat boy, she doesn't have a mother!" *(Back to us.)* Okay, actually, I say nothing. I've got this thing with confrontation. I once had to see a therapist to help me break up with my other therapist. Besides, is it really my job to educate them all? I never asked to be the poster boy for gay parenting. I just wanted a child. Growing up, it was never a question I'd get married and have a family. It wasn't till I was twelve, and my father couldn't get us tickets to *Annie* and I started hyperventilating on the kitchen floor, that it became clear that I probably wouldn't be marrying a woman. When my partner, Steve, and I decided to take the leap into parenthood, we'd been together eight years. That's like fifty-six in hetero-time. Our gay friends reacted in their typical low-key demeanor. *(Mock terrified.)* "A baby?! What are you thinking? You own a suede sofa from Armani Casa!" The straight folks were also supportive in … their way. One of them actually said, "Isn't it hard enough to raise a child in a normal family?" We crossed her off the godmother list. The first thing we had to do was find an egg donor and a surrogate. It's preferred if these are two different people. The agency we were working with soon matched us with a potential surrogate — Donna. A perky lesbian from Simi Valley. Healthy, a mother of two. Her profile said she wanted to help gay people become a family so she can show her kids the brave new world they live in. So, we have this very bizarre "first date" at Starbucks with Donna and her girlfriend and basically try to cover everything in two hours — "Where'd you go to school?" "Would you abort in the event of Down syndrome?" "Oh, we love *Xena: Warrior Princess*, too!" Six lattes later we're all jittery and love each other and agree to move forward. Next, it's time to begin our egg hunt. Every night Steve and I look at photos and read profiles. I fight for looks, he fights for brains — I remind him we live in Los Angeles. When our child isn't asked to her senior prom, he can sit in her room with her and do calculus. And just when we're convinced there isn't a candidate with the genetic makeup good enough for us, we find her. Donor 6247. A month later, sixteen eggs are extracted from this angel, and as per the agreement we never see or hear from her again. Steve and I are then called to the fertility center to do our part. We are escorted to separate "deposit closets" … or "masturbatoriums" … you get the idea … and this nurse hands me a specimen cup the size of a Big Gulp and tells me no water, no spit, no lube. Go! I start sweating. Two minutes later, Steve knocks on the door to tell me he's finished, and I tell him I'm freaking out and I need a little support. He tells me to hurry the fuck up 'cause our meter's almost out. What a good father he'll be. But the threat of a parking ticket does the trick, and I quickly finish up. Seventy-two hours later, we pick one lucky egg to transplant into Donna's womb. And then we hold our breath … for ten very long days. I'm at work when Steve calls. He's crying. Now, Steve cries when he watches a *Little House On The Prairie* re-run, so I'm not sure if we're pregnant or if Pa burnt down the barn. But then he gets it out — he says we did it — we're having a "gaby." We swear to each other we won't tell anyone for three months. We tell everyone that afternoon.

We talk to Donna at least two times a day. She is the most amazingly responsible person I know, yet every night, visions of her doing bumps of crystal meth at some rave party dance in my head. When we visit her I sneak into her kitchen and go through her garbage to make sure there aren't any empty cans of mercury-tainted tuna fish. I read on the internet that "oral sex may cause air embolisms that could result in spontaneous abortions," which I try to work into casual conversation. It's a long nine months. But we're in the home stretch. And my latest fear is what happens the moment this baby is born. I want to make sure the doctor knows to hand the baby to Steve and me, not to our surrogate. I become obsessed — we need to bond with the baby instantly. The baby comes to us. So, the big day arrives. Donna, her girlfriend, Steve and I sit in this hospital room. The nurses tell us everything looks good, nothing to do but wait. Four hours later, the contractions are a minute apart, and Donna's allowed to start pushing. At this point my inner asshole comes out and I whisper again to the obstetrician — the baby comes to us. Now, Donna originally had wanted us to stay up at her head while the baby was being born — which was fine with me. Saw one of those things in the Nineties, never need to see it again. But when the baby starts crowning, she yells, "Get down there! You can't miss this!" And as always, she's right. Steve actually helps catch our daughter as she's being delivered. Then the nurse wraps her in a blanket and I hold my daughter for the first time. I look up and see Donna watching us – sweaty, snotty, tears running down her cheeks — and once again, all plans out the window. I instantly hand the baby over for her to hold — as it should be. She wanted to make us a family. And she did. Sometimes we don't feel so different from everyone else … and other times it's "Where's your mommy?" And as I look at my now-three-year-old daughter, I realize it's my turn to show my child the brave new world she lives in. *(Christmas music fades back in.)* So, as she gets off Santa's lap, I turn to him and say *(To imaginary Santa.)* "Hey buddy, there is no mother. She doesn't have one. She just has two people who love her more than anyone ever could. And that's her Daddy and her Papa." My daughter pipes in, "That's what makes me special." And I think it couldn't get any better … but then I hear the little girl behind us burst into tears. And when her mother asks her what's wrong, she says, "I only have a daddy. I want a papa, too!" *(Smiles.)* Brave new world. *(Lights shift.)*

CHAPTER THREE: SEX TALK

SEX TALK FUGUE
by Michele Lowe

Actresses A, B, C and Salesman.

C. Charlene missed three days of school last week on account of the flu. She comes home after her first day back, and I say, "So what'd you miss?" and she says, "Daphne put a condom on a banana."

B. I hear Landon listening to Eminem on his computer, and as I walk in his room, I hear the word "clitoris."

C. So I say, "Was this at lunch?"

B. So I think: Is this a teachable moment?

C. She says, "Ma, don't be stupid. It was Sex Ed, and I heard the condom broke."

B. I ask him, "Do you know what a clitoris is?" And he says, "Um. Maybe."

A. I take my daughter Serena for her first bra fitting and the woman says we should come back when Serena has something "to offer" those are her words, "to offer."

C. So I ask: "Did they give her another condom? Did they let her try it again? Just because it broke doesn't mean she shouldn't use one." And Charlene says, "Ma relax, it was a banana, not a cock." A COCK she says.

B. How do you explain the source of a woman's sexual pleasure to a twelve-year-old boy?

A. So I pull this jerk saleswoman aside, and I say, "Honey I know they're small but she's only eleven. Can you show a little enthusiasm?"

C. So I go buy a bunch of bananas and a package of condoms.

B. So I do five minutes on clitorises, making sure to mention all 8,000 nerve endings, and he says "OK, thanks, you can leave."

SALESMAN. Trojans are on special. Two for one.

C. I don't care. These work, right?

A. I tell the saleswoman, "I'll pay you whatever you want just make her feel good about her breasts. They're little, they're perky, they're great. Say it. Say they're great."

SALESMAN. They're great, but a lot of women tell me they like the Twisted Pleasure or the Fire and Ice ones.

C. It's for a banana.

SALESMAN. *(Deadpan.)* What you've got is fine.

A. Finally, this woman digs out of the back of a drawer this little padded bra the size of a postage stamp and gives it to Serena, and her face lights up like a lightbulb.

C. While Charlene's in the shower I leave one banana and two condoms on her desk.

B. As I leave the room, I hear him call his friend Andy and say, "Hey don't play any Eminem at home. Never. *Ever.*"

C. Charlene is still in the shower when Amanda, my ten-year-old, comes out of Charlene's bedroom eating the banana. She hands me the condoms and says, "I think these are Dad's." *(Lights shift.)*

NOOHA'S LIST
by Lameece Issaq

Lights up on Aneesi, a woman of about 45. She reads from a paper in her hand.

ANEESI. I find this today in Nooha's room. "Brushes, soap, four remote controls." Tsk, four? No. *(Reading.)* "Chicken drumsticks ... drinking glass." The cat? *(She shakes her head.)* Lies! List of lies!

NOOHA. *(Offstage.)* No it isn't!

ANEESI. "Victims of Velocity: Things Mom Threw At Us While In A Fit of Rage, A Catalog of Madness."

NOOHA. Someone has to keep track! *(Beat.)* Ugh. This is gross.

ANEESI. Don't be scared, *habibti.* It's easy. Peel off the paper on the back, then put it on your underwears, then fold the wings down over the sides —

NOOHA. *(Offstage.)* I know, Mom! I saw Rula do it a hundred times. *(Beat.)* My God, I could float down a river on this thing! It's a friggin' raft!

ANEESI.   *Yallah,* go lay down and rest. And stay off of the Spaceface!

NOOHA. *(Offstage.)* Facebook, MySpace!

ANEESI. Whatever! *(Beat. Aneesi takes in the audience. She smiles.)* My daugher, the middle one, she just get her period. Late start, Nooha, she's 15. I get mine when I am 11. Eleven! Oof. Worst day of my life. Anyway. Tonight we're gonna have 50 people to the house for Iftar dinner and she get her period — I say, "Now? In the middle of Ramadan? I need help cooking!" She get her period just to get out of helping. I'm serious. My kids is very lazy. Rula, Romi, Nooha — they all sit in the same room on their labtops sending each other messages on the Tweet!

NOOHA. *(Offstage.)* Twitter. We Tweet on Twitter. Jesus.

ANEESI.   What Jesus have to do with it? Go lay down! *(Whispers to the audience.)* Sometimes when one of them leaves the computer on the MyFace, I look at it to see what all my kids doing — we live in Las Vegas! I don't want them to turn into prostitutes and gamblers. But, they good kids and they surprise me, you know? Like, this year Nooha wants to fast for Ramadan with the older kids. So cute. I tell her, no, *habibti,* never while you're bleeding. And oh my God, I never seen her so hysterical. She is crying — "I don't want this! I hate this! It makes me dirty." I say, "No! Dis don't make you dirty, maybe make you crazy. But dirty, no!" And she say, "Koran says!" I say, No. The Book doesn't mean that. Listen. What is the period? The egg — it is the potential for life. It is … eh, how you say … the energy of creation. So, the body, she need time to remove this energy that she doesn't need anymore. So, God give time off for the body to rest and the soul to rejuvenate. God is VERY, very smart. Okay? Once a month, a lady she get a mini-vacation. God say, "Listen, go and have a hot bath and eat an ice cream and two pounds chocolate. Don't fast, don't pray, don't do nothing but relax." I'm telling you, God, she is a woman. *(Beat. Aneesi looks at the list and shakes her head. Looks up at the audience and shakes the list.)* "Chicken drumstick … at Rula on September 9 because she said something rude at kitchen table. Nobody knows what. The cat … at Romi on October 9 for not picking up her poop. A remote control … at Nooha on November 9 for changing the channel to *Gossip Girls* while Mom was watching Al-Jazeera."

See, there are very good reasons! *(Beat.)* September ninth, October ninth, November ninth. Oh. I see. This is no list of madness, it's just PMS!

NOOHA. Oh, come on! *(Aneesi inspects the list again.)*

ANEESI. "Special note: Due to Mom's terrible aim, not one of these objects ever landed on its intended victim — " Oh really. I tell you good story. One time while I am 16 years old, I go to Nazareth to stay with my uncle's family for a few weeks. They live in an apartment on the top floor. And you know I have big, big crush on my cousin, Laith. Sounds weird, but it's natural. Everyone fall in love with their cousin. Anyway, I am on my period, and in my uncle's home there is one very tiny bathroom with one very tiny trashcan. Now, the pad is very, very big, and to wrap it in toilet paper it becomes like soccer ball. Huge! Will fill up the whole trash can! And of course, I am embarrassed by this — I don't want Laith to see. So, I just throw them out the bathroom window. A few days later my uncle screaming "Aneesi! Come here! You throwing your garbage into the neighbors garden? Shame on you!" They landed on the neighbor's head while he was in the garden picking mint!

NOOHA. *(Offstage.)* Oh my God! That is hilarious!!

ANEESI. I was mortified. But my *tayta*, my grandmother, she pull me aside and say "Good for you, Aneesi. Sometimes you have to remind a man that without a woman's suffering they would not exist!" She laughed for like half hour. She was like high priestess, this lady.

NOOHA. *(Offstage.)* Mom! Mommy … can you make me some tea? *(Aneesi looks up at the audience and smiles.)*

ANEESI. Be right there, *habibti. (She gets up to go, but pauses.)* For the record, I don't have bad aim. I miss on purpose. *(Lights shift.)*

MY ALMOST FAMILY
by Luanne Rice

A winter landscape.

WOMAN. I loved a man who had two daughters. I met the girls one winter in a boatyard, his sailboat in a cradle on dry land. Beth, fourteen, stood behind him, so still I could barely see her. Callie, twelve, leaned over the boat's rail, called, "Anyone down there want to come up and help me?" I climbed the ladder.

"Do you and my father kiss?" she asked. "Yes," I said. "Do you make out?" The pattern was set: She had a lot of questions, and I had a lot to answer for. While Duncan hadn't exactly left his wife for me, we were in a certain amount of gray area. It wasn't crystal-clear they would have split up if I hadn't come along. I wanted the girls to like me. That's a lie. I wanted them to love me. I asked my mother, "How do I do it?" She told me, "Don't try to be their mother. Cook them dinner, make everything they like and let them help with the salad dressing." I made steak and mashed potatoes, salad, chocolate cake. I lit candles and put out cloth napkins. Duncan mixed oil and vinegar before I could ask the girls, but even so, I thought we were doing all right. The dinner ended early; Beth had an asthma attack, had to go home.

Callie and I took rides in my old car. I let her shift gears while I worked the clutch, and she asked me to teach her to drive. "You bet, Cal — when you get older." We talked, and she had a million questions. Why didn't I have children of my own, why didn't I want to be a mother? *(She considers.)* To be a mother, you had to be stronger than I was, know more than I knew, be forever steady in a way I couldn't trust I could be. I told Callie: "I guess I'm just not cut out to be a mother." She said, "You'd be a good one. You're a good stepmother." Beth called me her step-monster. She wheezed gently, constantly, a little accordion of pain. Once, I wrapped her in a blanket, and she leaned into me. I held my breath, wanting everything to be better, to stay just like this. The wheezing got worse.

One summer, Duncan's cousin got married. The whole family went to the wedding. As we walked in, I saw the girls' mother. I grabbed Duncan's hand — but the girls ran toward her, pulling him with them. They stood in a tight knot — Duncan, the girls and their mother facing inward. I started toward them, but I couldn't see an opening. Beth stared across the tent at me — not with triumph, not with hate, just fear. Just the look of a young girl telling me that if I walked over, everything she loved in that moment, in her whole life, would stop. I felt shut out and illuminated all at once: They were each other's family, and I was just so tired of trying to force my way in. The next week, I taught Callie to drive a stick shift. And then I moved out.

This afternoon, Callie called from the emergency room. She's old enough now, she's gotten her license, had an accident, asked me to come get her. And I did. She has two black eyes and stitches on her forehead. They let her leave with me because she told them I was her stepmother. She asked to spend the night at my house, put off telling her parents about the car. I want her with me. But I know she needs to be with the people who've been with her forever, even before the beginning. I told her she couldn't stay, and I felt it dissolve, the dream of myself as something like her mom. I love her. So much so, I'd do anything for Callie, even send her home to her mother. Even that. *(Lights shift.)*

MICHAEL'S DATE
by Claire LaZebnik

My son tells me that a girl in his English class agreed to go to the
movies with him on Friday night, and I manage to say, "Oh?
Cool," in the most relaxed, unconcerned, hey-it's-your-life-not-
mine kind of way. I get her name out of him but not much more,
so I check out her picture on his Facebook page. She's actually kind
of cute. And, look — she commented on one of his statuses! "Ha-
ha. LOL." What a doll! I love her already. At bedtime, I pop a
Xanax along with my calcium and wonder if Michael's as nervous
about this date as I am. God only knows. I seriously doubt he'd talk
to me about his feelings. He's male, he's a teenager and he's autis-
tic. The perfect trifecta for emotionally shutting out your mother.
Friday night, Michael puts on a button-down shirt. I blow my hair
dry, dust on a little make-up, add a shpritz of perfume and spend
an hour trying to find something to wear that doesn't make me
look fat. I beam at Chloe when we pick her up. "Hey, there! How
ARE you? It's SO great to meet you!" "Uh, yeah, that's my mom,"
Michael mutters. They sit side by side in the back seat. I can't stop
glancing at them in the rearview mirror: Talk about cute — it's like
having two puppy dogs back there. I drive them to the cinema.
Hey, look at me! I'm dropping off my son and his date. His date!
Maybe this is the beginning of a whole new era for us. You see,
Michael was diagnosed with autism when he was three. He could-
n't talk or make eye contact, and he flapped his arms all the time.
I'd say it's miraculous that he goes to a regular high school now,
except I remember the billions of hours of speech and behavioral
therapy it took to get him there. And now he's on his first date. I'm
waiting at the movie theater forever — got there way too early —
but finally they're coming out side by side and heading toward the
car, and I'm peering at them, trying to see what their expressions
are, but I can't really tell. All I can see is that they're not actually
talking to each other at the moment, and that can't be a good sign
but maybe it's not a bad sign either, maybe it's a companionable
silence. When they get in the car, I ask how the movie was. Chloe
says she liked it. Michael says it sucked. He says that the lead

actress in it sucked and so did the music and the directing. Chloe says she thought the actress was really good. No, Michael says, that actress sucked, that actress always sucks. Chloe says no she doesn't, she's been in lots of good movies. Michael says you're wrong, they're all bad, and starts to list each and every movie the actress has ever been in, every one of which — you guessed it — sucked. I can see the expression on Chloe's face in the rearview mirror, and my heart sinks. "To each his own!" I cut in desperately. "So, Chloe ... tell me ... what does your dad do for a living?" She says he's a lawyer. "Oh, my God!" I say. "My dad's a lawyer too. That is an amazing coincidence, isn't it?" Michael, the kid who never makes eye contact, shoots me a disgusted look in the rearview mirror. "So who's ready for some frozen yogurt?!" I ask. "With way too many toppings? Let's make ourselves sick!" But Chloe says that she promised her parents she'd go straight home after the movies and just shakes her head when I offer to call them. We get to her house, and she jumps out of the car and quickly thanks us before slamming the door and racing away. "I probably should have kissed her goodnight," Michael says. "I'm not so sure," I say. "Why did you talk so much?" he says. "That was embarrassing." "I was trying to help you make conversation." "I didn't need your help. You ruined everything." "No, you ruined everything!" And instantly I try to take it away: "Oh, God, Michael, I'm sorry. I didn't mean that. You did fine, it was fine, really, she probably just had to go home early, like she said." He's silent. I grip the steering wheel hard and pretend that I have some control over where we're going. *(Lights shift.)*

CHAPTER FOUR: STEPPING OUT

GRADUATION DAY FUGUE
by Michele Lowe

Actresses A, B, C and C's Husband.

B. Three days before graduation! Three days!

C. My son's giving the valedictory speech, and I know he hasn't written it yet.

B. Sonia says she's not going to graduation.

A. Bridget tells me she wants to wear a bikini under her graduation gown — a little string thing.

C. Eric spends all day at the beach. He goes out all night with his friends.

A. "Does it have to be a bikini?" I ask. "Half the stuff you wear doesn't cover your ass anyway. Wear some of that."

C'S HUSBAND. Has Eric written his speech yet?

C. No. And don't bug him.

B. The first one on both sides to graduate high school and she won't go. I beg her. I plead with her. She says, "No way. You're making too big a deal."

A. I start getting phone calls from the other mothers. Am I letting Bridget wear a bikini under her gown? Whose side am I on? Jesus Christ, I gotta pick a side?

C'S HUSBAND. Has Eric written his speech yet?

C. No, and don't bug him.

B. I've been cooking for three weeks. I've got 65 people coming.

A. I get an email from the principal forbidding the girls to wear bathing suits under their gowns.

C. I should've forced him to write it last week.

A. This whole thing is driving me crazy.

B. This is crazy.

C. Crazy. The night before graduation Eric comes in my room and says he has no idea what to write.

B. I wake her up in the middle of the night and I say, "You tell me why you won't go. Tell me! Did you do something bad?"

C'S HUSBAND. Has Eric written his — ?

C. I'm working on it!

B. "Are they holding you back?" She says, "Don't be stupid." "Then what?" I ask. "Tell me please." She says, "You're all just too damn loud."

C. I ply him with Coca-Cola until finally around 2 A.M. he gets an idea and writes three completely different speeches. He reads them to me at dawn and each one is brilliant. Brilliant!

B. So we make a deal. She'll go to her graduation if Papi and I go alone. The next morning I tell everybody else not to come.

A. After breakfast I tell Bridget, "I'll make you a deal. You can wear a bikini under your graduation gown if I can wear a thong under my miniskirt."

C. Eric's speech was called "The Virtues of Procrastination."

A. She wore a dress.

B. Papi and I go alone to Sonia's graduation, and we sit there, and when they call her name I take out my cowbell and I ring it. Tough on her. *(Lights shift.)*

THREESOME
by Leslie Ayvazian

Rock music comes up. The music builds. Lights up on a Woman listening. When she talks to the audience, the music swells and she enjoys talking above it.

WOMAN. It's good, isn't it! *(Listens.)* My son. *(Listens.)* This is his! … And this is how we talked to each other! *(She yells.)* WHAT?

ACTOR (AS SON). *(Yells back.)* WHAT?

WOMAN. *(She yells.)* WHAT?! *(She returns to audience, music swelling.)* And it wasn't a phase! *(Referring to the music, she says.)* I like this part here. *(Listens.)* My husband and I were married for ten years before our son was born, and we became parents — proud, careful, older parents. We were a threesome, a dynamic threesome.

And despite all my ridiculous over-protection (like, my neighbor bought her son a skateboard and just let him ride it. I bought my son a skateboard and ran alongside it.) — despite things like that — my husband was patient and my son kept going. He created a world of his own. A musical world. This was the sound in our house from seventh grade on. This was the backdrop for everything else: school, friends, broken hearts, summer jobs, applying to college, selecting a college, and suddenly, wow, we were loading the van! … His guitar was the last thing he packed. The three of us drove up to school. Two parents in front, one young man in the back. We moved him in: drawers filled, bed made, posters up, his guitar and his amp next to his desk. We met his roommate: "Hello Hello." And then it was time to say goodbye. I didn't want to cry. I had worked on that — ten months in therapy his senior year. I wanted to hug him and give him a smile and let the tears come on the way back, which they did. It was a highway of tears, which sounds like a song. And then we were home. And then we heard this … *(Music has stopped.)* The quiet. *(She listens to the quiet.)* I thought I was prepared. But there were his old Converse sneakers by the front door. His *Guitar* magazines on the steps to his room. His socks on the landing. His toothbrush in the bathroom. HIS TOOTHBRUSH! "HE LEFT HIS TOOTHBRUSH!" I yelled to my husband. "I MUST BRING IT TO HIM."

ACTOR. *(As husband.)* "There are pharmacies in Rhode Island."

WOMAN. My husband said. Which is the case. I checked. My son is now 20 years old, a sophomore. And he's doing fine. School's good, band's good, friends are good. … And I'm fine. … But still, sometimes I hear myself talking out loud. "How are you, sweetie?" I'll say. "Do you need anything?" Then I wait.

ACTOR. *(As husband.)* "What are you waiting for, honey?"

WOMAN. My husband asks, quietly. "I'm waiting, I guess, to stop waiting." I say. And my husband says:

ACTOR. *(As husband.)* "You don't seem to want to do that."

WOMAN. And I say: "It's taking a while. That's all. … It seems to be taking a while." *(Lights shift.)*

BRIDAL SHOP
by Michele Lowe

FLORENCE. Pretty bridal shop.

RISA. Oh, yes. I think it's the nicest. We've been to all of them.

FLORENCE. First for me. Who are you waiting for?

RISA. My daughter. She's already picked out some dresses.

FLORENCE. My daughter-in-law's meeting me.

RISA. Your daughter-in-law included you? Wow.

FLORENCE. Lorraine's a lovely girl. Best thing that's ever happened to our son. He says it all the time. Best thing ever.

RISA. My son-in-law's a doll.

FLORENCE. Lorraine's a baker.

RISA. He's an attorney.

FLORENCE. We are so lucky.

RISA. We are. *(Beat.)*

FLORENCE. I'm never going to see my son again, am I?

RISA. Probably not.

FLORENCE. Is there anything I can do?

RISA. Well, there's a few things …

FLORENCE. Help me. Please.

RISA. Rule Number One: Give her space. Miles of it. You got advice you want to give her? Write it down and then burn it. Rule Number Two: She knows your son better than you do. She thinks that, he thinks that. Now EVERYBODY thinks that. Get used to it. Rule Number Three: Everything she does is fine with you.

FLORENCE. She makes chocolate chip cookies with happy faces on them.

RISA. You love those cookies.

FLORENCE. She wears knee socks with her dresses.

RISA. You love those knee socks.

FLORENCE. I don't think I like her. But I want her to LOVE me.

RISA. Good luck.

FLORENCE. There must be something I can do. I love my son.

RISA. He's hers now.

FLORENCE. You know this?

RISA. I know it for a fact.

FLORENCE. How?

RISA. How often does your husband see his mother?

FLORENCE. I'm going to be different. She's going to love me a lot.

RISA. You go, girl.

FLORENCE. You'll see.

RISA. She did invite you here. *(Beat.)*

FLORENCE. Lorraine doesn't know I'm here.

RISA. WHAT?

FLORENCE. I overheard her telling a friend of hers about the appointment, and I thought I'd surprise her and —

RISA. Oh my God.

FLORENCE. What should I do? She'll be here any minute.

RISA. I told you what to do.

FLORENCE. Now? That starts now?

RISA. Rule Number One!

FLORENCE. Torch my advice.

RISA. Rule Number Two.

FLORENCE. I don't exist …

RISA. And if you don't exist …

FLORENCE. I'm not here.

RISA. Right. *(Beat.)*

FLORENCE. To hell with the rules! They're archaic. They perpetuate the lack of communication between mothers-in-law and their daughters-in-law. They're bullshit. *(A doorbell rings.)*

RISA. Oh, look. A blonde wearing happy-face knee socks just walked in.

FLORENCE. Bye. *(Florence exits.)*

STARS AND STRIPES
by Jessica Goldberg

WOMAN. Day before he left for Afghanistan we got the same tattoo, a small blue star on our right shoulder. Probably seems like a weird thing for a mother and son to do together, or so my ex loves to tell me, "That's not right, no mother and son should be getting tattoos like that." But then, he didn't raise him, so what does he know? Last time Brian was home on leave he told me, "Mom, I seen things." And that made me really sad because, well, because you want to know the world your boy has seen, you know? You want to see it first. You know what I'm saying? Like, you want to be the one to always go first into the dark, make sure there's nothin' scary there, and if there is, you want to be the one to make it safe. So, it's just, it's just frustrating that you can't do that. 'Cause that's what a mother does, and knowin', knowin' you can't, well, that is hard. But, as my ex says, "Brian's a grown man, and you should be proud." Well, I am proud! So proud. I'm proud of all my children, but he's my soldier! Life on the line was never gonna be good enough for him, like it is for his daddy. Brian always wanted somethin' more. He was never gonna have no life of fixing windshield wipers onto trucks. After high school, Brian worked EMT for a while, but that still wasn't enough. Then one day he called me up so happy, "I found my calling, Ma," he said, "I joined the Army, I'm gonna serve my Country." Well, I just about fell off my chair, all I could think was: We are at war. You are going to have to go to war. He did three and a half months of basic training at Fort Carson and was gone. Now, working EMT in Detroit is no piece of cake. That keeps a mother up at night, but it is nothing like this. Nothing like this at all. This is like … constant. ALL THE TIME. From waking to sleeping, and sleeping, too, 'cause you're dreaming it. Half your time you spend trying not to look at the TV, at the newspaper, other half of the time you're like, why does no one care? Where is everyone? Then one day, there's a knock on the door. I'm standing in the kitchen when it comes, I'm fixing dinner, I hear it: the doorbell, the knock. There's three of them, that's how they come, in threes — two guys in dress greens and a chaplain. They come like that, and you know. My name, they're saying my name, then his, they're saying his name: Brian. What? Brian. I'm not prepared at all. I can't hear. There's water in my ears. I faint, I fall over, they tell me again: "Brian." That's when I rip their eyes out with my nails, with my teeth, I'm screaming. I want to go back in time. I want to stop time, but wait … Wait … This isn't real. It hasn't happened. I have to imagine it so that if it does happen I'm prepared. My ex-husband laughs when I tell him, "You're being a damn fool you know? Doting, TATTOOING?! Brian is 22 years old!" He laughs, laughs at me … *(Shakes her head.)* Well, you know what? F U. F F F U. 'Cause you see, I will do whatever it takes, whatever it takes: I will tattoo my back with stars, 22 stars, one for each year of his life. 23 stars, 24, I will tattoo and tattoo. 75 stars, 80 stars and he will live that long, and he will live and he will live. I will tattoo my back the whole night sky and nothing bad will happen, and he will live, and he will come home, hundreds of stars, and my soldier will come home! *(Lights shift.)*

CHAPTER FIVE: COMING HOME

THANKSGIVING FUGUE
by Michele Lowe

Actresses A, B, C and Actor D.

D. David drops a hint to our daughter Galina that maybe she should do Thanksgiving this year. Her dining room's bigger than ours. She says, fine she's game. She'll do it.

A. Isabel asks if she can bring her new boyfriend, Carl, home for Thanksgiving, and I say of course. We're gonna meet Carl! Get out the Lenox!

B. I don't do big Thanksgivings. All that pilgrim crap makes me itch so we do Chinese.

C. My son tells me he's not coming home for Thanksgiving this year. He's going to Cabo with a friend.

D. I decide Galina needs a little inspiration, so I take all my November issues of *Food and Wine* starting from 1998 and my three *Barefoot Contessa* cookbooks and my menu cards embossed with the little gold turkey and put them in a box.

C. The twins call and say they're not coming; they're going to a yoga conference.

A. Then Isabel tells me that I've got to buy organic sheets for Carl or he can't sleep in our house.

B. I rent two extra TVs, and we paint our faces and watch football and eat chicken chow mein on the snack trays, and I am in heaven.

C. My daughter's also not coming home for Thanksgiving; she's going to her mother-in-law's.

D. I copy all my recipes, 23 pages, and put them in the turkey box along with my mother's carving set and the antique chocolate turkey molds. I just want to be helpful.

C. Nobody asks what Mommy's doing for Turkey Day.

A. Isabel tells me Carl's a vegan. It's okay for him to see the turkey meat, but not the bones. So we have to carve it in the mudroom. Under a sheet.

B. After the last game, the kids will scatter like leaves and call me when they get home and say: "Mama that was the best Thanksgiving you ever made."

D. I'll make Thanksgiving next year. Or maybe I'll do a little one on Friday night after hers.

C. Nobody wonders if Mommy has any plans. Which I think is hilarious.

A. Carl better be gone by Christmas.

C. Because Mommy's had a plane ticket to Paris since August. *(Lights shift.)*

ELIZABETH
by David Cale

Bobby Barnes, a man in his early forties.

BOBBY. After my divorce became final I moved back in with my mom.

As part of the settlement my ex-wife got the house. Mom was living alone, and she'd said,

"Come and stay with me for a bit, it'll give you a little breathing space to figure out what you want to do with your life."

So I did.

She was standing on her doorstep when I pulled up in the car. The first thing she said to me was,

"I don't want to be called Betty anymore. I want to be called Elizabeth. That's my name, but everyone's always called me Betty, I don't know why. Elizabeth says something, Betty's just blah."

I said,

"Sure Mom, I'll call you Elizabeth."

And I hugged her hello.

Shortly after, I realized my mother barely went out.
I said to her,
"Why don't you go out anymore?"
She brushed me off.
"I like staying home."
"You're not being truthful, what's going on?"
"I'm a homebody now."
"Mom!"
Then she got really upset.
"I can't remember anybody's names! I get into a room full of people and I go blank. It's too stressful. And I can't remember things people have said to me from one week to the next! Oh, I don't want to talk about it, Bobby, please, subject closed."
In the night she tapped on my bedroom door.
"I'm sorry, sweetheart, how I shouted at you."
I said,
"There's no need to apologize, you're frustrated, I understand."
But I couldn't get to sleep thinking about it.

Living at home, I noticed the first thing my mother did in the morning was turn on the TV, and the last thing she did at night was turn it off, and she was now participating in it.

I walked in the house one evening and she was sitting in the armchair with her home phone in one hand and her cell phone in the other.
I said,
"What are you doing with those two phones in your hand, Mom?"
"Voting," she said, and she had a slightly guilty look in her eyes.
"What for?"
American Idol.
"Why do you need two phones?"
"I'm voting for *my David.* I've got both the phones on re-dial. I'm voting for him over and over. He's so talented, Bobby. And sweet. He's *got* to win. It's going to really upset me if he doesn't win."
"Mom," I said, "Do you have a little crush?"

She got all defensive.

"Don't be ridiculous, Bobby, I'm fifty-one years older than he is."

"Oh, so you've done the math? When you've finished voting for your boyfriend, I have an idea I want to talk to you about."

I sat her down at the kitchen table.

"Did you have lunch today?

"Of course I did."

"What did you eat?"

"I had a cookie."

"You can't live on cookies and TV. Mom, I think you're vegetating a little bit. No wonder you feel like you're losing your memory, you don't use your mind anymore. When was the last time you read?"

"I read!" she said.

"What? What was the last thing you read?"

"I read an article on whether Kirstie Alley's weight gain might be linked to Scientology."

"Mom, I have an idea. And don't just say no without considering it. I think you should go to night school. They have classes at the community college. There's one coming up on American Short Fiction. You used to love reading. And we have to get you on a better diet. I brought home some ginkgo biloba, it's good for the memory."

"Alright," she said, "Whatever you think best."

"I don't believe it," I thought, "She's going to do it."

I filled in all the forms and enrolled her as Elizabeth Barnes.

"I'm so happy I'm going to be Elizabeth again," she said, "it feels like a fresh start."

The first day of school arrived, and I couldn't get her out of the house. We had an absurd showdown in the kitchen.

"Elizabeth, get in the car."

"Why are you calling me Elizabeth? I'm your mother, call me Mom."

"You're going to be late for school. Please get your books and your bag and get in the car. And don't make faces at me."

"I don't want to go to school today, I'll start tomorrow."

"Mom," I said, "I've had a long day at work, please get in the car."

She had three hours of classes. I was a nervous wreck. I parked outside the college, and sat in the car waiting 'til she came out.

At nine-thirty she appeared, got in the passenger seat.

"Oh my goodness, I've got to read Sherwood Anderson's *Winesburg, Ohio* by Thursday. I haven't made it to the end of a book in twenty years. But I'm gonna do it. I am," she said, and she patted my leg.

I asked,

"How many people are in the class?"

She said,

"I don't know, six. Maybe eleven."

And didn't say anything else for the rest of the ride.

The following evening, we were in the kitchen.

She stood at the window looking into her yard. She went quiet for a long while, and seemed to be floating out into another world.

I asked,

"What are you thinking, Mom?"

She said,

"You know what I was just thinking, Bobby? I was just thinking, I don't want people to call me Betty anymore. My name's Elizabeth. People called me Elizabeth when I was a girl. But as soon as I became an adult I became Betty. I want to be Elizabeth again."

"Alright, Mom, I'll call you Elizabeth. Now sit up at the table and do your homework."

I thought,

"I can't move out. I can't leave her on her own."

She sat there reading, gently tapping her lip with a pencil.

I made us some dinner.

When I glanced back at her she was drawing cartoon birds in the margins of her notebook.

"Oh my God," I thought, "*I* used to do that at school."

(Lights shift.)

REPORT ON MOTHERHOOD
by Beth Henley

A sitting room in an old house in Hattiesburg, Mississippi.
A young girl interviews her great-grandmother for a school
report.

GREAT-GRANDDAUGHTER. *(Quietly.)* Great-Grandmother?
(Louder.) Great-Grandmother.
GREAT-GRANDMOTHER. What do you want?
GREAT-GRANDDAUGHTER. I wanted to ask you about moth-
erhood. For my report. I've spoken to Mother and Grandmother,
now if I speak to you that will be three generations of mothers.
GREAT-GRANDMOTHER. Oh, dear.
GREAT-GRANDDAUGHTER. I don't need much. I only have
a few questions.
GREAT-GRANDMOTHER. I'm very old. It doesn't allow me to
be superficial.
GREAT-GRANDDAUGHTER. Yes, ma'am. That's fine. You are
the mother of seven children. Four girls and three boys.
GREAT-GRANDMOTHER. All of them. Yes.
GREAT-GRANDDAUGHTER. *(Reading from paper.)* First of all,
what do you like most about being a mother?
GREAT-GRANDMOTHER. I don't like being a mother.
GREAT-GRANDDAUGHTER. You don't like motherhood?
GREAT-GRANDMOTHER. It's something I don't do well. I
don't love all my children the same. People say you should. But
I couldn't. Two of them I didn't like, one I despised. The one I
loved the most was quiet. Never spoke. A calm person, except for
the allergies and asthma attacks. We took the train to New
Orleans about those asthma attacks. The doctors scratched her
back with needles and put on various serums to see what she was
allergic to. It was legion. Grass, pollen, dust, the sun, the sky, her
own skin. She was my favorite. I cut her hair in a pixie cut. I cut
all my children's hair in pixie cuts. The girls, not the boys. The
boys' hair was even shorter. Children do not like washing their

hair, that is why they need less of it. And the tangles. I worried about knots and tangles. How do you feel about having children?

GREAT-GRANDDAUGHTER. I haven't given it a lot of thought.

GREAT-GRANDMOTHER. Do you use birth control?

GREAT-GRANDDAUGHTER. No.

GREAT-GRANDMOTHER. Why not?

GREAT-GRANDDAUGHTER. I'm twelve and —

GREAT-GRANDMOTHER. No sex.

GREAT-GRANDDAUGHTER. No. No. Hell, no.

GREAT-GRANDMOTHER. When I was your age, we didn't have the option. The option of premarital sex. Birth control was primordial and through it all I became very pregnant. I tried everything: the rhythm method, prophylactics, diaphragm, outside ejaculation, oral copulation, illegal abortion, abstinence. None of it worked. Now you have choice. Many choices. I can't tell you what a different world.

GREAT-GRANDDAUGHTER. That's good.

GREAT-GRANDMOTHER. Not entirely. Many terrible things are in this world. Apparently, civilization will end in an unfathomable and brutal fashion. In the meantime, I'm very happy for reliable birth control because we all want to be wanted.

GREAT-GRANDDAUGHTER. Yes. Of course.

GREAT-GRANDMOTHER. The happiest day of my childhood was when my own mother looked at me and said, "I forgive you, Cynthia." "For what? " I asked. "Because you have come uninvited into this household. Uninvited but eventually not unloved."

GREAT-GRANDDAUGHTER. What did she mean?

GREAT-GRANDMOTHER. She meant, eventually, I was loved. That's what I hope for everyone. It is not inevitable. Love. Did you know that, Helen?

GREAT-GRANDDAUGHTER. No. *(A beat.)* I don't think I want children. I don't want to be a mother.

GREAT-GRANDMOTHER. Good. You may decide as you like. I like your hair. How long it is, without tangles.

GREAT-GRANDDAUGHTER. I don't really like short hair on me.

GREAT-GRANDMOTHER. No. Why would you? You're young. How does it feel to be young?

GREAT-GRANDDAUGHTER. I have a boyfriend. But he doesn't know.

GREAT-GRANDMOTHER. Ah.

GREAT-GRANDDAUGHTER. He's shorter than I am.

GREAT-GRANDMOTHER. That could change. Have you spoken?
GREAT-GRANDDAUGHTER. I asked him what time it was.
He said he wasn't wearing a watch, but he smiled at me.
GREAT-GRANDMOTHER. Did you smile back?
GREAT-GRANDDAUGHTER. I guess … I did.
GREAT-GRANDMOTHER. You did? Good. *(Lights shift.)*

MY BABY
by Annie Weisman

I'm going to tell you this now, while it's fresh in my mind, because
I know how time creeps up on you. How it's just one day becom-
ing another, and then all of a sudden it's 35 years. You won't believe
that now, because you're not even a month old yet, but wait. So I
have to tell you now, what it was like, the day, the hour, the very
moment that you were born. This is how it happens. I'm eating a
brisket sandwich with your daddy and doing my dead-on impres-
sion of the hippy yoga teacher we just giggled through birth class
with, and we laugh and then, gush, my water breaks. And one
minute it's jokes and brisket, and the next minute we are driving to
the hospital, saying, but not believing, "We're gonna be parents." I
look at the car seat and its government-mandated five-point har-
ness in the back, and I try to fill it up with the idea of you, but fail.
It's impossible. No way this thing inside of me is a person. And
there are hours and hours at the hospital for it to get more real.
Contractions that get bigger and closer together, monitors that
show your heart beating away, but still, it's impossible to believe.
How will it happen? After the epidural, there's no pain to distract
me anymore from the impossible task at hand. It's 2 A.M., your
father is asleep in a vinyl chair, and I am alone with beeping
machines, ice chips and paralyzing fear. And this goes on for hours
until at last I'm dilated 10 centimeters and they page the doctor.
He breezes in just before 5 A.M. sipping a large latte and pulling a
crisp white lab coat over a worn T-shirt. Just another ordinary day
for him. He had time to stop at Starbucks for a latte. I can't stop
shaking. The nurse whispers to the doctor, "She's panicking." And
he takes his place on a wheeled stool at the foot of the bed, his face

framed by my trembling legs. He places a hand on my leg — authoritative but gentle. "Annie, here's what you're going to do. You're going to hold your legs up like this. You're gonna take a deep breath, and let it out. Then you're gonna take another deep breath and hold it, and that's when you push. Push as hard as you can. Push exactly like you're having a bowel movement. But don't worry, you won't have a bowel movement. You'll have a baby. Ready? Deep breath." Of course, I know this is coming, this moment when they tell me it's time to push out my baby. And yet, YOU HAVE GOT TO BE FUCKING KIDDING ME. Why don't you just tell me to SPEAK RUSSIAN, or FLY. There is no way. No WAY. And still, I do it. I hold my legs back, take a deep breath and let it out, take another breath, hold it and push as hard as I can. Nothing happens. The doctor says, "Annie. You aren't really pushing. You need to push with everything you've got." And I want to kick out his sweet authoritative teeth. I know this is how it's done but I can't do it. I can't do it. I do it again. "That's it, Annie! That's great! Now do it again." And I can't, but I do it again, and again until the doctor says, "The baby is crowning, no more pushing, just relax and I'm going to bring the shoulders out so you don't tear, and I'm going to hand her to you but very gently because she's still connected inside you, and here she comes, here she comes," and I'm still thinking no way, there's no way, it's not a person, and then "Here she is!" And oh my god! You are in my arms, and you are, you are a person, warm and wet, with bones and hands, and swollen little eyes darting back and forth, and you see me and I see you and we both cry, you, a dry, rhythmic little wail, and me an overwhelming flood of love and relief. "Hello my darling. Hello my baby." Later, they take you off for tests with your daddy, and I have a moment by myself to relive what just happened. You landed on my chest and took your very first breath. The morning sun moves across the vinyl floor of the hospital, and the next thought comes to me. If you could begin to breathe before my very eyes, you could stop too. As sure as you were just born, someday, you are going to die. And it could happen any second.

A week later my mother visits. And it takes her less than five minutes to piss me off. She starts with passive aggressive questions "Shouldn't she have gained more weight by now? Are you sure that swaddle isn't too tight for her to breathe?" and transitions to full blown irrational diagnoses: "She's jaundiced. She's lethargic." "Mom, she's a newborn, and she's tired." When she offers a ride to the emergency room, it gets ugly. "Mom! I saw the pediatrician this morning, and he says she's small, but she's fine, and we don't need the emergency room and we don't need you here undermining my confidence, and — " But before I can finish, my mother bursts into tears. "You don't understand. You're still my baby. It hasn't been 35 years, it's been 35 minutes and you just came out. I'm sorry, but … you're my baby." Later, I hold your tiny body in my arms and rock you in the glider until long after you're fast asleep. I keep rocking until I'm not angry at my mother anymore.

I want to tell you this story now, even though you can't possibly understand it. I want you to know why I love you so much more than you will be able to tolerate someday. Because however old you are, ten, twenty, seventy … there was still a moment, years ago, that I'll never forget. When one second you weren't there, and the next second you were. Life began. And I got to be there. *(Lights fade to black.)*

End of Play

PROPERTY LIST

Bed sheet
Blanket
"Happy looking" diaper bag
Diaper bags
Cigarette, lighter
Shopping bag with gifts
List
Kotex with "wings"

SOUND EFFECTS

Baby gurgle
Baby cry
Holiday Muzak
Rock music
Bell

NEW PLAYS

★ MOTHERHOOD OUT LOUD by Leslie Ayvazian, Brooke Berman, David Cale, Jessica Goldberg, Beth Henley, Lameece Issaq, Claire LaZebnik, Lisa Loomer, Michele Lowe, Marco Pennette, Theresa Rebeck, Luanne Rice, Annie Weisman and Cheryl L. West, conceived by Susan R. Rose and Joan Stein. When entrusting the subject of motherhood to such a dazzling collection of celebrated American writers, what results is a joyous, moving, hilarious, and altogether thrilling theatrical event. "Never fails to strike both the funny bone and the heart." –*BackStage*. "Packed with wisdom, laughter, and plenty of wry surprises." –*TheaterMania*. [1M, 3W] ISBN: 978-0-8222-2589-8

★ COCK by Mike Bartlett. When John takes a break from his boyfriend, he accidentally meets the girl of his dreams. Filled with guilt and indecision, he decides there is only one way to straighten this out. "[A] brilliant and blackly hilarious feat of provocation." –*Independent*. "A smart, prickly and rewarding view of sexual and emotional confusion." –*Evening Standard*. [3M, 1W] ISBN: 978-0-8222-2766-3

★ F. Scott Fitzgerald's THE GREAT GATSBY adapted for the stage by Simon Levy. Jay Gatsby, a self-made millionaire, passionately pursues the elusive Daisy Buchanan. Nick Carraway, a young newcomer to Long Island, is drawn into their world of obsession, greed and danger. "Levy's combination of narration, dialogue and action delivers most of what is best in the novel." –*Seattle Post-Intelligencer*. "A beautifully crafted interpretation of the 1925 novel which defined the Jazz Age." –*London Free Press*. [5M, 4W] ISBN: 978-0-8222-2727-4

★ LONELY, I'M NOT by Paul Weitz. At an age when most people are discovering what they want to do with their lives, Porter has been married and divorced, earned seven figures as a corporate "ninja," and had a nervous breakdown. It's been four years since he's had a job or a date, and he's decided to give life another shot. "Critic's pick!" –*NY Times*. "An enjoyable ride." –*NY Daily News*. [3M, 3W] ISBN: 978-0-8222-2734-2

★ ASUNCION by Jesse Eisenberg. Edgar and Vinny are not racist. In fact, Edgar maintains a blog condemning American imperialism, and Vinny is three-quarters into a Ph.D. in Black Studies. When Asuncion becomes their new roommate, the boys have a perfect opportunity to demonstrate how open-minded they truly are. "Mr. Eisenberg writes lively dialogue that strikes plenty of comic sparks." –*NY Times*. "An almost ridiculously enjoyable portrait of slacker trauma among would-be intellectuals." –*Newsday*. [2M, 2W] ISBN: 978-0-8222-2630-7

DRAMATISTS PLAY SERVICE, INC.
440 Park Avenue South, New York, NY 10016 212-683-8960 Fax 212-213-1539
postmaster@dramatists.com www.dramatists.com

NEW PLAYS

★ **THE PICTURE OF DORIAN GRAY by Roberto Aguirre-Sacasa, based on the novel by Oscar Wilde.** Preternaturally handsome Dorian Gray has his portrait painted by his college classmate Basil Hallwood. When their mutual friend Henry Wotton offers to include it in a show, Dorian makes a fateful wish—that his portrait should grow old instead of him—and strikes an unspeakable bargain with the devil. [5M, 2W] ISBN: 978-0-8222-2590-4

★ **THE LYONS by Nicky Silver.** As Ben Lyons lies dying, it becomes clear that he and his wife have been at war for many years, and his impending demise has brought no relief. When they're joined by their children all efforts at a sentimental goodbye to the dying patriarch are soon abandoned. "Hilariously frank, clear-sighted, compassionate and forgiving." –*NY Times*. "Mordant, dark and rich." –*Associated Press*. [3M, 3W] ISBN: 978-0-8222-2659-8

★ **STANDING ON CEREMONY by Mo Gaffney, Jordan Harrison, Moisés Kaufman, Neil LaBute, Wendy MacLeod, José Rivera, Paul Rudnick, and Doug Wright, conceived by Brian Shnipper.** Witty, warm and occasionally wacky, these plays are vows to the blessings of equality, the universal challenges of relationships and the often hilarious power of love. "CEREMONY puts a human face on a hot-button issue and delivers laughter and tears rather than propaganda." –*BackStage*. [3M, 3W] ISBN: 978-0-8222-2654-3

★ **ONE ARM by Moisés Kaufman, based on the short story and screenplay by Tennessee Williams.** Ollie joins the Navy and becomes the lightweight boxing champion of the Pacific Fleet. Soon after, he loses his arm in a car accident, and he turns to hustling to survive. "[A] fast, fierce, brutally beautiful stage adaptation." –*NY Magazine*. "A fascinatingly lurid, provocative and fatalistic piece of theater." –*Variety*. [7M, 1W] ISBN: 978-0-8222-2564-5

★ **AN ILIAD by Lisa Peterson and Denis O'Hare.** A modern-day retelling of Homer's classic. Poetry and humor, the ancient tale of the Trojan War and the modern world collide in this captivating theatrical experience. "Shocking, glorious, primal and deeply satisfying." –*Time Out NY*. "Explosive, altogether breathtaking." –*Chicago Sun-Times*. [1M] ISBN: 978-0-8222-2687-1

★ **THE COLUMNIST by David Auburn.** At the height of the Cold War, Joe Alsop is the nation's most influential journalist, beloved, feared and courted by the Washington world. But as the '60s dawn and America undergoes dizzying change, the intense political dramas Joe is embroiled in become deeply personal as well. "Intensely satisfying." –*Bloomberg News*. [5M, 2W] ISBN: 978-0-8222-2699-4

DRAMATISTS PLAY SERVICE, INC.
440 Park Avenue South, New York, NY 10016 212-683-8960 Fax 212-213-1539
postmaster@dramatists.com www.dramatists.com

NEW PLAYS

★ **BENGAL TIGER AT THE BAGHDAD ZOO by Rajiv Joseph.** The lives of two American Marines and an Iraqi translator are forever changed by an encounter with a quick-witted tiger who haunts the streets of war-torn Baghdad. "[A] boldly imagined, harrowing and surprisingly funny drama." –*NY Times.* "Tragic yet darkly comic and highly imaginative." –*CurtainUp.* [5M, 2W] ISBN: 978-0-8222-2565-2

★ **THE PITMEN PAINTERS by Lee Hall, inspired by a book by William Feaver.** Based on the triumphant true story, a group of British miners discover a new way to express themselves and unexpectedly become art-world sensations. "Excitingly ambiguous, in-the-moment theater." –*NY Times.* "Heartfelt, moving and deeply politicized." –*Chicago Tribune.* [5M, 2W] ISBN: 978-0-8222-2507-2

★ **RELATIVELY SPEAKING by Ethan Coen, Elaine May and Woody Allen.** In TALKING CURE, Ethan Coen uncovers the sort of insanity that can only come from family. Elaine May explores the hilarity of passing in GEORGE IS DEAD. In HONEYMOON MOTEL, Woody Allen invites you to the sort of wedding day you won't forget. "Firecracker funny." –*NY Times.* "A rollicking good time." –*New Yorker.* [8M, 7W] ISBN: 978-0-8222-2394-8

★ **SONS OF THE PROPHET by Stephen Karam.** If to live is to suffer, then Joseph Douaihy is more alive than most. With unexplained chronic pain and the fate of his reeling family on his shoulders, Joseph's health, sanity, and insurance premium are on the line. "Explosively funny." –*NY Times.* "At once deep, deft and beautifully made." –*New Yorker.* [5M, 3W] ISBN: 978-0-8222-2597-3

★ **THE MOUNTAINTOP by Katori Hall.** A gripping reimagination of events the night before the assassination of the civil rights leader Dr. Martin Luther King, Jr. "An ominous electricity crackles through the opening moments." –*NY Times.* "[A] thrilling, wild, provocative flight of magical realism." –*Associated Press.* "Crackles with theatricality and a humanity more moving than sainthood." –*NY Newsday.* [1M, 1W] ISBN: 978-0-8222-2603-1

★ **ALL NEW PEOPLE by Zach Braff.** Charlie is 35, heartbroken, and just wants some time away from the rest of the world. Long Beach Island seems to be the perfect escape until his solitude is interrupted by a motley parade of misfits who show up and change his plans. "Consistently and sometimes sensationally funny." –*NY Times.* "A morbidly funny play about the trendy new existential condition of being young, adorable, and miserable." –*Variety.* [2M, 2W] ISBN: 978-0-8222-2562-1

DRAMATISTS PLAY SERVICE, INC.
440 Park Avenue South, New York, NY 10016 212-683-8960 Fax 212-213-1539
postmaster@dramatists.com www.dramatists.com

NEW PLAYS

★ **CLYBOURNE PARK by Bruce Norris.** WINNER OF THE 2011 PULITZER PRIZE AND 2012 TONY AWARD. Act One takes place in 1959 as community leaders try to stop the sale of a home to a black family. Act Two is set in the same house in the present day as the now predominantly African-American neighborhood battles to hold its ground. "Vital, sharp-witted and ferociously smart." *–NY Times.* "A theatrical treasure…Indisputably, uproariously funny." *–Entertainment Weekly.* [4M, 3W] ISBN: 978-0-8222-2697-0

★ **WATER BY THE SPOONFUL by Quiara Alegría Hudes.** WINNER OF THE 2012 PULITZER PRIZE. A Puerto Rican veteran is surrounded by the North Philadelphia demons he tried to escape in the service. "This is a very funny, warm, and yes uplifting play." *–Hartford Courant.* "The play is a combination poem, prayer and app on how to cope in an age of uncertainty, speed and chaos." *–Variety.* [4M, 3W] ISBN: 978-0-8222-2716-8

★ **RED by John Logan.** WINNER OF THE 2010 TONY AWARD. Mark Rothko has just landed the biggest commission in the history of modern art. But when his young assistant, Ken, gains the confidence to challenge him, Rothko faces the agonizing possibility that his crowning achievement could also become his undoing. "Intense and exciting." *–NY Times.* "Smart, eloquent entertainment." *–New Yorker.* [2M] ISBN: 978-0-8222-2483-9

★ **VENUS IN FUR by David Ives.** Thomas, a beleaguered playwright/director, is desperate to find an actress to play Vanda, the female lead in his adaptation of the classic sadomasochistic tale *Venus in Fur.* "Ninety minutes of good, kinky fun." *–NY Times.* "A fast-paced journey into one man's entrapment by a clever, vengeful female." *–Associated Press.* [1M, 1W] ISBN: 978-0-8222-2603-1

★ **OTHER DESERT CITIES by Jon Robin Baitz.** Brooke returns home to Palm Springs after a six-year absence and announces that she is about to publish a memoir dredging up a pivotal and tragic event in the family's history—a wound they don't want reopened. "Leaves you feeling both moved and gratifyingly sated." *–NY Times.* "A genuine pleasure." *–NY Post.* [2M, 3W] ISBN: 978-0-8222-2605-5

★ **TRIBES by Nina Raine.** Billy was born deaf into a hearing family and adapts brilliantly to his family's unconventional ways, but it's not until he meets Sylvia, a young woman on the brink of deafness, that he finally understands what it means to be understood. "A smart, lively play." *–NY Times.* "[A] bright and boldly provocative drama." *–Associated Press.* [3M, 2W] ISBN: 978-0-8222-2751-9

DRAMATISTS PLAY SERVICE, INC.
440 Park Avenue South, New York, NY 10016 212-683-8960 Fax 212-213-1539
postmaster@dramatists.com www.dramatists.com